David Nut

Dr. Johannes Faustus

A puppet play now first done into English- in four acts

David Nut

Dr. Johannes Faustus
A puppet play now first done into English- in four acts

ISBN/EAN: 9783743322592

Manufactured in Europe, USA, Canada, Australia, Japa

Cover: Foto ©Thomas Meinert / pixelio.de

Manufactured and distributed by brebook publishing software
(www.brebook.com)

David Nut

Dr. Johannes Faustus

Mediæbal Legends.   No. I

Dr. JOHANNES FAUSTUS

PUPPET PLAY

NOW FIRST DONE INTO ENGLISH

IN FOUR ACTS

LONDON
DAVID NUTT IN THE STRAND
1893

PREFACE

Dr. Johannes Faustus' Puppet Play though last in order of time, takes the first place in this collection of Mediæval Legends on account of the supreme interest attached to it as source and inspiration of Goethe's Tragedy. Let not the reader, however, expect to find Goethe or even Marlowe anticipated in this ancient relic of another spirit and another age. This Faustus is no tragedy, artistically antique or philosophically modern, but a Puppet Play pure and simple, which as popular "Morality" still bears traces of the earlier stage of ecclesiastical "Mystery." Ignorant and careless alike of Art this dramatic version yet obeys many of Art's canons. In marked contrast with the loosely or wholly unconnected incidents of the Prose Legend (Note No. 7 of this collection), from which Marlowe formed his plot, the Puppet Play presents strict unity of design, stern necessity with relentless irony of Fate and unflagging action on the part of characters which, if crudely drawn, are yet well sustained and perhaps gain in colour what they lack in shade, while the essentially Mediæval and Teutonic weird mingling, in familiarity bold but *not* profane, of sublimity and buffoonery, of the super and the cynically natural, so utterly at variance with Grecian harmony, was well calculated to inspire pity and terror in an audience to whom the scene depicted no poet's fancy but the intense reality of life here and hereafter.

Accept then, Reader, in the spirit of their own time and not of ours, these last words of the Middle Ages, as acted so lately as 1844, for the last time in Europe by Schütz and Dreher's Kasperle Company at Berlin.

DRAMATIS PERSONÆ

Dr. Johannes Faust.

Christoph Wagner, *his Famulus.*

Duke of Parma.

Duchess of Parma.

Don Carlos, *Seneschal at Court of Parma*

Casperle, *Faust's Servant, afterwards Night-watchman.*

Gretl, *his Wife.*

Mephistopheles ⎫
Auerhahn
Astarot
Megära
Haribax   ⎬ *Evil Spirits.*
Polümor
Asmodeus
Vitzliputzli
Xerxes   ⎭

Faust's Guardian Angel.

Two Women, *one young, one old.*

King Solomon ⎫
Samson and Delilah
Judith and Holofernes ⎬ *Apparitions.*
David and Goliath
Helen of Troy ⎭

SCENE—*Alternately* Mainz *and* Parma.

ACT I.

SCENE I

FAUST *in his study, seated at a table laden with folios.*

FAUST.

I've now arrived at such a pitch of learning,
That to a laughing stock for men I'm turning ;
All books I've searched, from preface to conclusion
And still, the Philosophic Stone, to my confusion,
I fail to find. My learning is in vain,
My labour brings but hunger, want and pain !
No decent coat is left upon my back.
Of all things but of debt, I suffer, pinch and lack.
Those sleepless nights, who will repay to me,
That vainly I devoted to Theology?
Away, then, Law and Medicine's idle fancy,
Henceforth I'll put my trust in Necromancy,
And, entering into compact with the Devil,
Learn Nature's secret from the Powers of Evil !
But e'er I reach this consummation tragic,
I must become an adept in the Art of Magic.

VOICE TO THE LEFT.

Woulds't thou wise and happy be,
Choose Magic; leave Theology.

VOICE TO THE RIGHT.
Faus   Heed not Magic's tempting voice,
But make Theology thy choice.
FAUST.
Voices around me on each side I hear,
To which shall I listen, to which give an ear?
I will question them both, then give judgment aright ;
So, tell me thy name, oh thou Voice on my right !
VOICE TO RIGHT.
The Spirit that guards thee.
FAUST.   So each one may say.
Now, there on my left hand, who art thou, I pray?
VOICE TO THE LEFT.
I am sent by Inferno's great Monarch to bless
Thee with gifts of perfection and pure happiness.
FAUST.
And were't thou the Devil's own kinsman, yet still
Thou art welcome, if only thou work me my will.
So accepting the Left and refusing the Right,
I shall reach the perfection of earthly delight.
VOICE TO LEFT.   Ha, ha !
VOICE TO RIGHT.   Thy poor soul !
FAUST.   It mislikes me to hear
How the Bad Spirit laughs, while the Good drops a tear.
But enough ! 'Tis my Famulus, now, who draws near.

SCENE II.
FAUST.   WAGNER.

WAGNER.
Pardon, Magnificence, the intrusion; I come

from the Post, which brought no letters, but three students, who desire to present a Treatise to your Magnificence.

FAUST.

Wagner! Go, tell these students that I take no more such treatises; I am weary of labour that turns my brain and earns not daily bread.

WAGNER.

Pardon, and permit me to point out that this is no doctor's dissertation, to be refuted or maintained by your Magnificence. It is a printed pamphlet, whose title, as I caught it at a passing glance, runs thus : " Clavis Astarti de Magica."

FAUST.

How! What ! Speaks an angel by you, or are these words of mockery?

WAGNER.

Magnificence ! I mock you not!

FAUST.

Go, Wagner, go ! Fetch in the students and serve them with the best. Give them wine and spice.

WAGNER.

Good ! Magnificence.   [*Exit* WAGNER.

FAUST.

Ha ! Now has Fortune become my friend ! The prize, so long, so vainly sought, shall be my own ! Where have I not asked? To what school of learning have I not applied for that very book which nowhere was to be found? Ye Spirits of Inferno, dwellers in Tartarus, tremble before Faustus, for now will he force you to declare your deepest mysteries, and to yield up those hidden treasures that have too long mouldered in the bowels of the earth !

WAGNER [*returns*].

Magnificence ! The students are below, and here is the book they brought.

FAUST.

Thanks, good Wagner, a thousand thanks ! Now am I happy, for Fortune smiles, and soon shall this wretched tenement be exchanged for a palace. Ah ! in what changed tones will the world soon speak of Dr. Faust ! What profit have my studies brought ? Of what avail that midnight poring over books ? Wagner, press them out, and if from those folios and those quartos you can squeeze one drop of living wisdom, why—I'll sell myself to the Devil !

WAGNER.

I would I saw our fortunes mend, but meanwhile may I ask a favour of your Magnificence?

FAUST.

Ask, but be brief.

WAGNER.

It is for leave to take a helper in the rougher work, that so I may have freer time for study.

FAUST.

Surely, good Wagner, you shall have a help; only be prudent in your choice, for I like not chatterers about my house—one thing more, if any ask for me to-day, say that I am out.

WAGNER.

Good, Magnificence! but would you not admit the students, who knowing you to be within, might haply wish to see you ere they go.

FAUST.

If needs must, let those students in.   [*Exeunt.*

SCENE III.

Enter CASPERLE *with knapsack.*

CASPERLE.

How pleased my Herr Papa would be to see me now. He always used to say, " Casperle, take care to set your affairs agoing," and, sure enough, here they go, sky high [*tosses knapsack in the air*]. Ha! Now I were provided for ten years to come if I did but need nothing for twenty. First of all [*proudly opening knapsack*] here is a brand-new coat. The stuff and lining, to be sure, still lie in the shop, but I've but to send the money, and presto! straight from the piece, stuff and lining will be cut and buttons thrown in all complete. Next, comes a pair of boots—soles and uppers are, of course, at the shoemaker's. Joking apart, it's desperate work seeking service and finding no master. Here have I been for half an eternity on the hunt for a place, and if I go on much longer the very soles of my feet will be worn out ; and as to hunger, I could

devour the mountains were they solid pies, and
drain the Mediterranean even if it were pure champagne ; but, Mord bataillon ! this calls itself an inn,
and yet I see no jug, no glass, no wine, no beer and
no waiter, so here's for a row.   Heida ! Waiter !
Landlord ! Valet ! Boots ! Chambermaid !   The
whole lot of you—Héda, here's an arrival !"

SCENE IV.

CASPERLE.   WAGNER.

WAGNER.

What's all this noise about ?   Friend, who are
you, and why do you make such a heathen din ?

CASPERLE.

Listen ! it's to your profit. Pray is it the fashion
here to keep guests waiting, who are hungry and
thirsty and haven't a penny in their pockets ?

WAGNER.

Friend, you are mistaken ; this house is not an
inn. If for money you would have food and drink,
go next door.

CASPERLE.

How ! is this no inn, and does one here get
nothing for one's money when one hasn't got any ?

WAGNER.

Friend, as I said, for what you want apply nex
door.

CASPERLE.

So you give no one food for money ?

WAGNER.

No ! I told you, no !

CASPERLE.

Well, well, I'm easy going, and, if needs must, I'll take a meal for nothing. Had I money, I would pay, but it doesn't matter, I don't mind [*sits down to table*]. Just serve all you have in the house, and were it double as much, I don't care if a button flies.

WAGNER [*aside*].

Poor simpleton, one can't help pitying his ignorance. Had he studied, he wouldn't be so light-hearted ! The more I learn, the less I laugh. Why not kill two birds with one stone by engaging him at once as servant and joke cracker. [*To* CASPERLE.] Look here, friend, it's all nonsense about the dinner, but by listening to reason you may earn a bit of bread. I want a servant and think you'd suit. The place is easy, for my master, His Magnificence Dr. Faustus, grudges nothing to me, who am his right hand, or so to say, his Alter Ego.

CASPERLE.

No ; it won't do.

WAGNER.

Why not? Don't throw away such a chance.

CASPERLE.

Why not? I'll soon tell you why not.

WAGNER.

Well? Let me hear.

CASPERLE.

It's right enough about the bread, even if there

were cake thrown in as well, but the place does 't
suit, because I want a master.

WAGNER.

That you can find in me.

CASPERLE.

Paperlapapp! That's just what I can't find in
you ; you're a servant, and it's a master I want.

WAGNER.

How do you know that I am a servant?

CASPERLE.

How do I know? Well, just guess; but as you
don't look like a Town Councillor I'll tell you.
Didn't you speak of your master? He who has a
master is a servant, and a servant is what I don't
want.

WAGNER.

Don't stick at that. For though I have a master,
I may need a servant; but if you like it better, I'll
take you into my master's service.

CASPERLE.

That's more like the thing ; only what about wages?

WAGNER.

My master offers twenty gold florins a year.

CASPERLE.

Twenty gold florins ! Not enough, I can't do the
work at the money, I must have at least six-and-
thirty pence.*

WAGNER.

A year?

* Groschen, 1⅓ penny Prussian.

CASPERLE.

Yes, a year ; year by year ; each year that it please God to send upon the land. That's my figure, and below it, with the best of will, I couldn't go.

WAGNER.

Why, you stupid ! I offer you more ; you cheat yourself. Just look here. One gold florin is worth more than six-and-thirty pence, and I offer you twenty florins, or if you still don't see I'll give you a present of six-and-thirty pence upon the bargain. Is that right ? Twenty gold florins wages, and six-and-thirty groschen down?

CASPERLE.

No, no ! That won't do. I'll drive as hard a bargain as I can. It must be six-and-thirty pence wages, and twenty gold florins down to drink. If not, good day ; do as you please. Dixi.

WAGNER.

What a simpleton ; but I must yield. Logic's lost on fools and children All right. I agree to your terms, but you must keep the matter quiet.

CASPERLE.

I can keep things quiet, especially when I don't know them ; but now drive up with the dinner, for I'm too hungry to dine off the sight of your milksop face.

WAGNER.

The kitchen's outside—go there to be fed.

CASPERLE.

I don't want to be fed, I want to eat.

WAGNER.

Then go to the kitchen, and there you'll get what you want.

CASPERLE [*goes off singing*] :

"From turnips and from sauerkraut
And home, I ran away,
Had mother roasted meat, no doubt
She might have made me stay."

ACT II.

SCENE I.

FAUST *alone. Afterwards* SPIRITS.

FAUST.

Strange ! The students have disappeared, and are nowhere to be found. All the same, I have their book, and being alone, can herewith begin the study of Magic. [*Opens book and reads.*] Ah ! That is how it is done ; nothing could be simpler, and yet I have puzzled over it for years ! [*Looses his girdle, lays it on the ground in a circle, enters circle.*] Now I will summon the spirits. [*Waves his wand, murmuring unintelligible words; crowd of spirits appear in the form of hairy apes.*] Here they come, thick and fast ; but which shall I choose, and how ? By their pace, I think ! Here ! you with the white horns, what is your name ?

SPIRIT I.

Vitzliputzli !

FAUST.

Say, how swift are you?

VITZLIPUTZLI.

As the snail in sand.

FAUST.

Ha! At that rate I need no spirits. Back whence you came. Apage, Male Spiritus! Next one! Who are you?

SPIRIT II.

Polümor.

FAUST.

Declare your pace.

POLÜMOR.

'Tis that of falling leaves.

FAUST.

At a pinch I could put on that pace myself. Hence! Apage, Male Spiritus! Next one! What name?

SPIRIT III. Asmodeus!

FAUST.

This may be my man! How swift are you?

ASMODEUS.

As falls the rushing cataract, so I fly.

FAUST.

Yet not fast enough! Back! Apage, Male Spiritus! Vivat sequens! Who are you?

SPIRIT IV.

Astarot!

FAUST.

May Nomen be Omen! And pace?

ASTAROT.

I am swift as a bird of the air.

FAUST.

Good ! but yet not enough. Apage, Male Spiritus.
Redhead ! Tis now your turn ! Your name !

SPIRIT V.

Auerhahn.

FAUST.

How swift art thou ?

AUERHAHN.

As the bullet, so I fly !

FAUST.

Still better, but not good. Apage, Male Spiritus.
Blue foot, thy name ?

SPIRIT VI.

Haribax !

FAUST.

And pace ?

HARIBAX.

'Tis the wind's !

FAUST.

Good pace, but yet too slow for me. Apage, Male
Spiritus. Two yet remain. Say ! Sooty Sweep !
Thy name ?

SPIRIT VII.

Megära.

FAUST.

And how swift ?

MEGÄRA.

As the Pest !

FAUST.

Ah, true! The Pest is swifter than the wind, yet sure, the last is best. Ultimus! Declare thy name.

SPIRIT VIII.

Mephistopheles!

FAUST.

How swift art thou?

MEPHISTOPHELES.

As Human Thought.

FAUST.

Done with you! As Human Thought! What more could I desire than to behold shaped in fulfilment my rising Thought? Why God Almighty can no more. Eritis Sicut Deus! Will you serve me?

MEPHISTOPHELES.

If Pluto but permit.

FAUST.

And who may Pluto be?

MEPHISTOPHELES.

My Master.

FAUST.

Go! ask your Lord to let you serve me eight-and-forty years, hereafter, I will be your bondsman; but come again in human form. I like not apes, and standing in this circle wearies me. Tell your master, too, that I demand to taste of every earthly joy, and to possess fair presence and great fame; true answer, likewise, I must have to every question.

MEPHISTOPHELES.

In a moment I am here again. [*Disappears*,

returning in human form, clothed in scarlet garments, covered by a long black cloak, and having a horn on his forehead. FAUST *steps out of circle.*]

MEPHISTOPHELES.

Your demands are granted by my Lord; but four-and-twenty years are the longest term of service for which I may engage.

FAUST.

Four-and-twenty years! Sure that means many a happy day and night. Good! I accept!

MEPHISTOPHELES.

If so, give me a little bond—for Life and Death.

FAUST.

If you must have it then, in black and white, fetch ink, for that in my horn has long been dry.

MEPHISTOPHELES.

Not black but red on white. Your signature alone is needed; the bond itself is ready written out, Optimâ Formâ, fair and clear; your signature in blood completes it. See! here's a needle, prick your finger with it.

FAUST.

Produce the bond, ere signing, I would read.

MEPHISTOPHELES.

Mercurius, appear! [*A raven appears with the bond in its bill.*]

FAUST [*takes and reads.*]

I, Johannes, Dr. Faustus, Professor, make the following agreement with Mephistopheles:

I. To abjure God and the Christian Faith.

II. After four-and-twenty years, reckoning 365 days to the year, to become his bondsman.

III. During these four-and-twenty years, neither to wash, nor to shave, nor comb my hair, nor to cut my nails.

IV. To foreswear marriage.

FAUST.

Strange! These two last and least conditions seem the hardest. Now—but why pick and choose? I'll take them as they stand, one with another.

MEPHISTOPHELES. Then sign ; here is a pen.

[*Gives crow-quill from his hat*

FAUST.

Freely my blood shall flow upon this day
When to thy Lord my soul I sign away.
Behold the ruddy stream, which seems to brand
In scarlet letters, flaming on my hand.
Great H and F that all too plainly say
From the impending doom " Homo Fuge ! "
Yet! F might stand for Faust and H for Honour great,
But whether fickle Chance it be or fixèd Fate,
I may no longer stand in doubt and hesitate.
The deed is signed, is sealed, repentance were too late
Yet I would clasp the parchment, but that o'er me creep
Strange languors of a faint and death-like sleep.

[FAUST *falls asleep in his chair.* GUARDIAN ANGEL *appears in form of* CHILD ANGEL, *bearing palm branch. Exit* MEPHISTOPHELES.

GUARDIAN ANGEL.

Misguided soul ! framed for eternal bliss,
How may I see thee sink in Hell's abyss ?

[FAUST *awakes. Exit* ANGEL.

FAUST.

What ! Am I then alone ? and do I wake from sleep ?
Refreshed I rise, and fearless meet my fate.
Spirit ! Appear ! Thou hast the charge to keep
In never-ceasing service on my will to wait !

MEPHISTOPHELES.

'Twas while in sleep forgetfulness you sought,
I left you.   Think ! Behold me with your thought
As pledged !

FAUST.   This paper take.

MEPHISTOPHELES.   Swift thro' the air
To Pluto shall Mercurius your message bear.

[*Raven flies away with deed in its bill.*

FAUST.

Your name, I think, is Mephistopheles ?

MEPHISTOPHELES.

On earth it is ; if so your Lordship please.

FAUST.

Hark ye, then, Mephistopheles ! You have indeed
appeared in human form, but that scarlet clothing
showing beneath your black mantle has an ill-look,
betraying you as a subject of the Powers of Darkness,
and with the horn on your forehead you cut a figure
that is simply unpresentable.

MEPHISTOPHELES.

Be easy ; only to yourself do I thus appear ; to the

world's eyes I seem whatever you may wish ; just as to human view, you, yourself, though as by compact neither washed nor kempt, shall ever be the fairest of mankind.

FAUST.

Good! but whither now away; no moment longer will I stay in Mainz, where, if gifted with Solomon's wisdom, none would heed me, because I'm a Professor.

MEPHISTOPHELES.

My cloak will bear us to the Court of Parma, where the Duke holds marriage festival. There you may revel in delights and gain fame and honour by your Magic Art, nor shall love adventures fail ; would you have your household go?

FAUST. Leave Wagner, for he wearies me.

MEPHISTOPHELES. But Casperle?

FAUST.

He may come, but not with us ; I've this and that to ask you on the way that is not for his ear.

MEPHISTOPHELES.

Away, then! In a few moments we shall be at Parma. [*Exeunt.*

SCENE II.

Enter CASPERLE, *stumbling over* FAUST'S *girdle, which lies still on the floor.*

CASPERLE.

Pardautz! Here I go taking the room's measure

by my own.   No good beginning ; but what indeed
have I met but bad luck upon worse ever since
I entered this rat's nest of a house.   Hardly had I
eaten through the bill of fare, than it and I seemed
to turn to empty space, and I had fain set to afresh.
And the rats !   *What* rats ; each a yard long, and
such beards !   They come and snatch the very bread
out of one's mouth.   Here I go again over one of
their tails.   Let's see, what is it ?   A tailor's measure ?
Has my master been tried on for a new coat, or
is he, himself, the tailor ?   I'll pocket it, as it'll do
for taking the length of the next prize rat I meet.
Still, my master can hardly be a tailor, for what
could a tailor do with so many books ?   Can't all be
fashion prints ?   There's one on the table, I'll look
at it.   [*Turns over pages.*]   Ah ! a Breviary, for
saying one's prayers out of ; that settles the matter
—my master's no tailor.   [*Reads.*]   K. K. Katz—
Pudel—or whatever it calls itself.   Queer work
reading is when one can't spell.   I'd have learned
spelling if only my grandmother hadn't died when I
was but a child of twenty ; still let's try what can be
made out.   Katz—Pudel—that's sure and certain.
Capital I.   That stands for "Schnapiter," First
Schnapiter.   Now we're getting on swimmingly
[*Reads.*]   "If—one—will — summon—spirits — one
says—Perlippe !   [*Crowd of spirits appear.*]   You
rats' tails, do you set up as spirits ?   What d'ye want ?
SPIRITS.
      To serve you.

CASPERLE.

Serve me! Well, what have you cooked to serve?

SPIRITS.

Steel and iron—Pitch and sulphur?

CASPERLE.

Then the deuce may dine with you, for I won't. [*Reads on.*] If—one—will—dismiss—spirits—one—says—Perlappe! [*Spirits vanish.*] All right! Off go the rat tails. It's an easy trade being exorcist. Perlippe! [*Spirits appear.*] Perlappe! [*Disappear.*] Works as smooth as grease! Now I'm a passed wizard! Queer creatures for God Almighty to have created. Now let's see what they can do! Perlippe! here, you rat's tail, what's your name?

SPIRIT I.

Asmodi.

CASPERLE.

A-la-modi! And how old may you be?

ASMODI.

Three thousand years old.

CASPERLE.

Nearly out of Modi; what can you make?

ASMODI.

Nothing, I undo others' work.

CASPERLE.

That's always something; but I don't quite take your word for it. Here's a chilblain on my toe. Can you take it away?

ASMODI.

Yes! If you pledge me your soul.

CASPERLE.

Ah! ha! you're a sharp fellow. Nothing for nothing, eh? Still, you're a dull Devil not to set to work better. Now, I'm tired of you, old Stick-in-the-Mud. There's a nice, bright, little Devilkin, no bigger than my hand, I'll speak to him! What's your name, old man?

DEVIL.

Xerxes.

CASPERLE.

Xerxes! Let's see! Surely that was an invincible general who took lessons in running away. And how old may you be?

XERXES.

Eight hundred and ninety-eight.

CASPERLE.

Indeed! So young! and already sprouting a beard. Ah, by keeping your eyes open you may come to something some day; only take my advice. Give up oversleep and nips of brandy, they stunt the growth. I know it by sad experience on my mother's dog, Mops. Ugh! you rascals, you reek like the pest; off with you. Perlappe. [*Spirits vanish.*] No! they shan't get off so easily; here goes, Perlippe! [*Spirits appear.*] Perlappe! [*Disappear.*] Perlippe, Perlappe, Perlippe, Perlappe, Perlippe, Perlappe, Perlippe. [*Repeats the words as quick as possible, till quite out of breath, stops with Perlippe. Devils, to avenge themselves, tie a rocket to his pigtail.*] There! I have kept them on the go; but who hunts others tires himself. [*Devil creeps up*

from behind, sets fire to his pigtail. Explosion.
CASPERLE *falls screaming to the ground, where he
remains as dead, long after explosion is over.*]

AUERHAHN [*shaking* CASPERLE].

Up, Casperle! Up! your master is off to Parma;
would you like to go there?

CASPERLE.

Parma! What could I do at Parma?

AUERHAHN.

Join your master, of course. Where the master
is there should the servant be also. Perhaps you
don't know that your master has sold himself to the
Devil.

CASPERLE.

Has he? What the Devil did he mean by it?

AUERHAHN.

If you like, I'll take you.

CASPERLE.

Where? To the Devil? I'm there already, for
you are here; if I hadn't been told you were the
Devil, I could guess, I've such a keen nose.

AUERHAHN.

It's not to the Devil that I'll take you, but to
Parma, where your master is revelling in delights;
for four-and-twenty years we spirits have to serve
him, and I am sent to bring you to him.

CASPERLE.

All right, take me, but don't be too long on the way.

AUERHAHN.

We'll go quick as cannon shot.

CASPERLE.

Put to, then.

AUERHAHN.

Already done. [*Fiery Dragon appears.*] Mount !

CASPERLE.

Oh, I say ! Who would grow old must live long. Do you mean to say that I'm to ride that Hell-Sparrow to Parma.

AUERHAHN.

Yes, indeed ! if you pledge yourself body and soul to me.

CASPERLE.

Fare charged besides ! I thought you had my master's orders to fetch me? [AUERHAHN *rubs his nose.*]

CASPERLE.

Any way you're out in your reckoning ; the thing's a pure impossibility.

AUERHAHN.

I don't see the impossibility.

CASPERLE.

Don't you? Well, look here ; my body I need myself, for I can't travel without it ; and as to a soul, what dummies of devils you are not to see that Casperle hasn't got one. When I came into the world the article was scarce.

AUERHAHN.

Well, well ! Up with you, it will be all right ; but just one thing more. Can you hold your tongue ?

CASPERLE.

Always, when I've nothing to say !

AUERHAHN.

Your master needs a silent servant, so, if you are not that, here you stay !

CASPERLE.

If that's all required, I'll chain up my mouth and put a padlock on it, but Apelpo ! I'm not going to skip any of my five meals.

AUERHAHN.

Five meals ! How do you get them all in ?

CASPERLE.

This is how you do it. A light early breakfast, and a late heavy one, a hearty midday dinner, a good supper, and later in the evening just a trifle of roast meat and salad, with a couple of pints or so of red wine.

AUERHAHN.

What can we keep you going on all the day long ?

CASPERLE.

Why something to eat, of course ?

AUERHAHN.

Mount, then ; but not one word on the way, that you may prove yourself no chatterbox.

CASPERLE.

All right. [*Mounts the Dragon,* AUERHAHN *gets up behind, and Dragon flies away.*]

ACT III.

SCENE I.

[Garden in front of Ducal Palace at Parma].

THE SENESCHAL, DON CARLOS. CASPERLE.

DON CARLOS, SENESCHAL.
When shall I see the end arising,
Of waste and drink and gormandising?
From balls and plays and masquerading
To take some rest there's no persuading.
Our Duchess, who, as one demented,
Each night fresh fancies has invented ;
H. H. has a right to congratulation,
But none to cause me such irritation.
For some new device in vain I batter
My wretched brain, for being a matter
Of fact individual, and no magician,
I'm "au bout de mon Latin" an awkward position.
But, by my staff official, my Star and Garter !
What do I see in the heaven's fore-quarter
But a golden-tailed and fiery dragon ;
That for sure were somewhat to brag on.
Ah ! Had I but known beforehand,
I'd have invited the Court to look on from a Grand
    Stand.
CASPERLE [*falling from sky at feet of* DON CARLOS].
    Just so ; here I lie, low enough. Truly the
fellow's as good as his word, but it's mean of him,

when I did but ask leave to speak now that we were
at Parma; just wait though, and see if I don't pay
him off some fine day.

DON CARLOS.

Bless me ! The clouds are raining down a stranger,
Who drops in, fearing neither hurt nor danger.
Sure ! one accustomed to take dragon exercise,
Has power the Spirits both to call and exorcise.
Such luck, at beck and call of pat arrival,
Marks me of Fortune's favourites the fit survival.
For, tragic knot, antiquity has surely never seen a
Worthier loosed, than this of mine, by Deus ex
    Machinâ.
So courage, to address the stranger, only courage,
Is all I need, who never needed Borage.*
My learned Sir.

CASPERLE.

Oh dear ! for sure, that's the Duke's self ; never
in my life have I had to speak to such a great man ;
but I'm not afraid !

DON CARLOS.   'Tis with some hesitation,
I dare inquire your name and habitation
Likewise——

CASPERLE [*trembling*].

Who's afraid ! Not I, Sir ! Not I !

---

* "Borage." This plant when eaten was supposed in the
Middle Ages to inspire courage, hence the saying, " Ego Borago,
animum do." " I, Borage, give courage." The reader will, it is
hoped, excuse this rather wide paraphrase of the original, " Ich
bin doch sonst nicht von den Blöden."

DON CARLOS,

If Spirits come and go at your citation?

CASPERLE.

Ah! my gentleman thinks that I can't hold my tongue, but I can, my good Sir, I can; and if I hadn't known how before, I've learnt it now. [*Rubs his elbow as though smarting from fall.*]

DON CARLOS.

You may place unbounded confidence in me.

CASPERLE.

Now, he's trying to pick my brains, but *I'm* not the man to tell him, as he wants to know, that my name is Casperle, and that I've come flying after my master, who's gone to the Devil. No! No!

DON CARLOS.

That's enough for the present ; so you are but the servant ! What's your master's name?

CASPERLE.

Why, look ye, that I mayn't say, I'm forbidden.

DON CARLOS.

But, what if I promise you a good tip?

CASPERLE.

Promise ! I tell nothing to promises; but give and you'll get.

DON CARLOS.

Take that, then.

CASPERLE.

Now, what I mayn't say, I'll show [*Holds up his clenched fist*]. German Faust !

DON CARLOS.

Faust! What does that mean?

CASPERLE.

Don't you take it in yet, pudding-head?

DON CARLOS.

If your master's name be Faust, I do. Ah! Faust, Dr. Faust! I've heard of him, I think. He comes surely from Maguntia, and if so, must be well versed in Magic.

CASPERLE.

He's not from Maguntia; he comes from Mainz; but is there no baker's shop at hand?

DON CARLOS.

Whither away so fast? I won't let you off without showing me a specimen of your art; for, from such a master, you have surely learned something worth seeing.

CASPERLE.

Learned something! Not I! Do me justice.

DON CARLOS.

Denial is useless; did not mine own eyes behold you riding through the air on Behemoth?

CASPERLE.

It wasn't Behemoth; it was a sparrow from Inferno.

DON CARLOS.

Where's the difference! Don't refuse, I'll pay what I see.

CASPERLE.

H'm! what shall I show you? Would you like to

see a *tremendous* deluge pour down and swallow us both up?

DON CARLOS.

Decidedly not ; that would be most dangerous, something else if you please !

CASPERLE.

Or shall I strike fire out of the ground, that will consume us both to ashes?

DON CARLOS.

That, too, were a serious matter.

CASPERLE.

Or would you like a millstone to fall upon you from the sky and bury you ten thousand fathoms deep in the earth?

DON CARLOS.

I can see perfectly well that you are making game of me ; I'll have nothing to do with such break-neck adventures. All I want is a nice drawing-room piece, than entails no danger, at least not on myself.

CASPERLE.

Then look out, for I'm going to fly away, sky high, so far away over the clouds and out of sight that you'll never see me again. Will that please you

DON CARLOS.

Yes ! I'd like to see that well enough.

CASPERLE.

Then keep your eyes open ; but, Apelpo ! pre-payment please, as I'm not coming back.

DON CARLOS.

Ah ! in that case don't go, for I must take you to my

Lord; all the same, take this [*Gives money*], and show me something else.

CASPERLE.

At that rate, you'll get what you please out of me. Now, here goes, a very, choice performance, a sight for sore eyes, it's so fine! [*Twirls round on his heel.*] Did you see

DON CARLOS.

No! I saw nothing.

CASPERLE.

That's just what there was to see.

DON CARLOS.

But I must see something.

CASPERLE.

Must you? Then do it yourself, for I can't.

[*Exit.*

DON CARLOS [*looking after* CASPERLE].

That's a jackanapes, but here comes His Highness.

SCENE II.

DUKE *and* DUCHESS *and* TRAIN *come along the terrace.*

DUKE.

Sweet Consort! Hold not in such light esteem
My love, as one short, fleeting week to deem
Enough for wedding joys, which would not seem
Too long, if flowing in an endless stream,
For, what so sweet in life as Love's young dream.

C

DUCHESS.

   My soul's a-weary of the glare and noise,
   'Tis but Love's still, small voice that Love enjoys;
   But, if needs must, let fireworks' dazzling show
   Be flaming signal of Love's inner glow.

DUKE.

   Such emblem were too fleeting, false and fitful
   Of love, which in its nature is immortal ;
   But here comes one, well fitted to give counsel,
   The longest head in Parma, our wise Seneschal.

DON CARLOS.

   I thank your Grace for such kind condescension,
   In praising my poor overtaxed invention.
   Her wish our Duchess shall, on intimation,
   Behold, fulfilled in airy conflagration.
   Nor even this exertion shall exhaust us,
   For a new-comer, one, named Dr. Faustus,
   Will give a show, though one proviso made is,
   That he is not to terrify the ladies.

DUCHESS.

     Why should we fear?

DON CARLOS.

               Because this great Magician
   Holds spirits loosed or bound at requisition.

DUCHESS.

     Delightful ! Bid him come !

DON CARLOS.

              To that, there is a hindrance,
   That none of us know where the sorc'rer made his
      entrance.

As yet, I have but seen and made entreaties fervent,
To one who's standing there and calls himself Faust's
   servant.
      [CASPERLE *appears, but, on being noticed,*
      runs away.

DON CARLOS.
   He flees.

DUCHESS.
   Pursue!
      [DON CARLOS *chases* CASPERLE *who,*
      refusing to be caught, runs repeatedly
      across the stage, DON CARLOS *after him.*

DON CARLOS.
   You rogue, I'm out of breath, 'tis scandal.

DUCHESS.
   My Lord! arise and help! The game is worth
the candle. [*Duke lays down his crown on bench and
joins* DON CARLOS *in pursuit of* CASPERLE.]

SCENE III.
FAUST. MEPHISTOPHELES. THE FORMER.

MEPHISTOPHELES.
   You're playing hide and seek. Our coming is
intrusion.

DUCHESS.
   Ah no, if you would speak, say on to the conclusion.

MEPHISTOPHELES.
   My master, Dr. Faust, far-famed for Necromancy.

DUCHESS.
   I've heard of him.

FAUST.

      Fame here exceeds my hope and fancy.

MEPHISTOPHELES.

  Soon all the round world o'er, men will say and sing
    his praises.

DUCHESS.

  Sure ! he's the master who the spirits calls and raises.

FAUST.

  The ring of Solomon ensures me their obedience.

DUCHESS.

  Pray show us of your art, though black are its
    ingredients.

FAUST.

  Fairest of women, fain would I obey,
  If such things could but be in light of day.

MEPHISTOPHELES.

    What matter where the sun, since day and night
  obey you.

FAUST.

    Ah, true, it shall be done.

DUCHESS.

    One moment, Sirs, I pray you. Now cease that
  jackanapes to chase thus faster and faster. For while
  you seek the man, see ! I have found the master, great
  Dr. Faust himself. Duke over all the Spirits !

FAUST [*aside*].

  She ranks me with herself according to my merits.

DUCHESS.

  He'll crown our wedding feast with honour and
    renown.

MEPHISTOPHELES.
  And his Grace's crownèd head will freshly now
    recrown.
DUKE [*resuming his crown*].
  Herr Doctor, pray come in. I'm still quite over-
    heated.
DUCHESS.
  The play will now begin ; so please let all be seated.
FAUST [*waving magic wand*].
  Daylight depart. Make way for stilly night.
  [*Night comes on.*] Now, say! what shall I bring
    before your Grace's sight?
DUCHESS.
  If choice then be allowed, show on his lofty throne,
  Him, to whom Spirits bowed : the wise King Solomon.
FAUST [*waving wand as before*].
  Behold the Monarch as he lived and moved.
                    [SOLOMON *appears enthroned.*
DON CARLOS.
                            Quite charming.
DUCHESS.
  I'd pictured him as gallant; not stern nor so alarming.
FAUST.
  The scene is changed, behold !
            [SOLOMON *appears, kneeling before* QUEEN
              OF SHEBA.
DUCHESS.
            Who is that lovely creature?
DUKE.
  Your very self.

DUCHESS [*aside*].
                    And *He* is Faust in every feature.
FAUST.
    Balkis her name, and she was Sheba's Queen,
    Before her greater wisdom, bowed, the King is seen.
    Another now.
DUKE.
    Not yet, this has such beauty—
DUCHESS.   Charm and grace.
FAUST.
    'Tis but a faint reflection of your lovely face.
DUCHESS.
    Surely she spurns not him, who prone before her lies
    Now, say, if you can read my wishes in mine eyes.
FAUST.
    Why not ?   Look up and say if I have read aright.
                        [SAMSON *and* DELILAH *appear*.
DUCHESS.
    Samson and Delilah, lovers, meet my sight.
DUKE.
    But where the shears ?
FAUST.
    A spirit truth divines, for it appears,
    She ne'er betrayed him to the Philistines.
DUCHESS [*aside*].
    Again my likeness ; and himself the giant.
    The rogue, no wonder, that of truth defiant,   .
    He likes not mention of the tell-tale shears.
    [*Aloud*]. Another !

FAUST. Do you choose what now appears.

DUCHESS.

No! choose yourself, for I find choosing *très ennuyeux.*

[FAUST *waves wand, Assyrian camp appears, with* JUDITH *beheading* HOLOFERNES.

DUKE.

Ah, Judith! fair again. Holofernes. H'm—might be *mieux.*

DON CARLOS.

She's taking off his head; it wasn't worth the sparing.

DUCHESS [*aside*].

My husband and myself! I find that rather daring.

Yet Faust is well enough to be had for the refusing.

[*Aloud*]. Another, if you please, and let it be amusing.

FAUST.

Think what you will, and see your thoughts arise.

[*Waves wand.* GOLIATH *and* DAVID *appear.*

DUKE.

Nor the big man nor the little do I call a great surprise.

DON CARLOS.

Goliath strikes too high, that's why he can't hit David,

Who takes him in the leg. Well done! That *was* a brave hit.

The giant's down! Now at him! While in vain for help he clamours,

See David with the sword, how he saws and how he hammers,

Off comes the head !   'Tis big as gourd bottle with
    thin gullet,
David sticks it with the trunk—into his shepherd's
    wallet,
That's surely not at all according to the Scripture.

FAUST.

Tis History here, not Holy Writ ; between them is
    a rupture.

DUCHESS [*aside*].

While others idly gaze upon the show,
The Sorcerer's hidden meaning, I, alone, can know.
To secret murder and forbidden love
He seems to point. Be this the test to prove,
The world must surely deem Lucretia pure ;
If held in like esteem, I am secure.

FAUST.

Your Grace's choice is made.

DUCHESS.

                Yes !   Show what I have willed.

FAUST.

Lady !   I have as yet your every wish fulfilled.

DUCHESS.

    Fails now your art?

FAUST.

              No empty shadows met your eye,
'Tis what your Grace has thought that lacks reality,
Lucrezia lived indeed—but—as a Borgia.*

---

* Reader will again excuse rather wide paraphrase in marking
point of original. " Lucretz had wohl gelebt, doch nie Lucretea."

DUCHESS [*aside*].
Well parried, Sorcerer.   His lie to forge, he a
Truth undeniable melts down to fable.
[*Aloud.*] If then, no empty shades, we should be able
To touch the pictures that you here present.
FAUST.
Lady !   To do so were your detriment.
DUCHESS.
Then, what I may not touch, I'll no more see.
FAUST.
Lady !   It rests with you, what yet may be.
DON CARLOS [*coming out of hall*].
Dinner is ready, may it please my Lord.
DUKE [*To* FAUST].
We pray you, as our guest to grace the board,
And hope, still later on, more sights to see.
FAUST.
Sir ! I will ever serve you readily.

    [*Exeunt* DUKE, DUCHESS, TRAIN ; FAUST
       would follow, but MEPHISTOPHELE
       holds him back by cloak.

MEPHISTOPHELES.
Follow not.
FAUST.
And why ?
MEPHISTOPHELES.
Flee from the court, for dear life, flee away !
FAUST.
What mean you ?

MEPHISTOPHELES.

Be advised by me.   Flee, if you love your life.

FAUST.

Why these false alarms, and what the danger?

MEPHISTOPHELES.

Threefold the danger is.   First from the Duke. His Grace's jealousy is roused, and he would poison you at table.

FAUST.

For that you'll find an antidote.

MEPHISTOPHELES.

High Dignitaries of the Church will sit at table, so I care not to be present.

FAUST.

Brave hero you!   What next?

MEPHISTOPHELES.

The Inquisition is on your track, to boil you in oil for contradicting Holy Writ.

FAUST.

First beheaded—then hanged—what next?

MEPHISTOPHELES.

Casperle, your servant, has set Hell in an uproar and Parma by the ears with Perlippe and Perlappe, so the mob is raising hue and cry against you, his master, as a conjuror of alarms and poisoner of wells.

FAUST.

Against prince, people and clergy, all banded together, I cannot stand, so away!   The Duchess only I regret, nor think that she will gladly see me go!

MEPHISTOPHELES.

I will give you Empresses for this Duchess. So now away to Constantinople.

FAUST.

Casperle I'll leave behind, lest he play his tricks again upon me ; but though forced let our departure be at least triumphant, to irritate the pudding-headed mob.

MEPHISTOPHELES [*aside*].

For that, I'll put myself to no extra charge.

> [CASPERLE'S *Dragon appears*, FAUST *and*
> MEPHISTOPHELES *mount, it flies away.*

SCENE IV.

CASPERLE *alone; after* AUERHAHN.

CASPERLE.

Mordblitz-kreutz-bataillon sapperment. If that isn't my Infernal Sparrow I see up aloft, and on it, forsooth, my Herr Master and his ourang-outang of a private, special devil-in-waiting. Pretty doings to leave me here in the lurch among the macaroni-gobblings ; really, it's beyond a joke. Héda ! Hé ! Take me too. Hé ! it's dinner-time ! They're as deaf as posts. Now what in the world am I to do among these Italian numskulls? I could cry like a sea-cat, if that were any good ? Shall I lead a bear or go about with marmots.

> "Avecque si, avecque la,
> Avecque la marmotte."

I might sell ink or rat-traps as Italians do with us ;
but then, where's the ink? Better turn vivandière,
for work never fails that trade. I have it ! Shows
the good of book learning. Perlippe, Perlippe,
Perlippe.

AUERHAHN.

Hold your noise, can't you? Here I am already.

CASPERLE [*embracing and kissing* AUERHAHN].

Pet of an Auerhähnikin, how glad I am to see
your black devil-face again.

AUERHAHN [*struggling to free himself from* CAS-
PERLE'S *endearments*].

Ugh-gh-gh ! you're choking me. Be done, can't
you? If you call a devil you must give him work.

CASPERLE.

Ah, darling Rat's Tail, my master's gone ; take
me to him !

AUERHAHN.

Your master has washed his hands of you as a
chatterbox.

CASPERLE.

Then just you put me where you found me.

AUERHAHN.

I've lost my horse, your master's gone off on it to
Constantinople.

CASPERLE.

Why, that must be in Turkey !

AUERHAHN.

That's an " Anachronismus "; in Turkey it's called
Stamboul.

CASPERLE.

To be sure, so it is ; I learnt and knew and forgot that again. Well, get another mount.

AUERHAHN.

Yes, in exchange for your soul.

CASPERLE.

Blockhead ! Haven't I told you that where there are no assets, the Emperor has no case.

AUERHAHN.

Well, well, out of pity I'll take you back to Mainz. But what will you do when you get there?

CASPERLE.

I read in the papers that the night-watch is dead, and I wan't to apply for his place ; it's easy, one can snore through the live-long day.

AUERHAHN.

And prowl about at night. It's all one to me Having brought you, I've got to take you back.

CASPERLE [*aside*].

Don't I always fall on my feet? He's got to take me back.

AUERHAHN.

That's all the thanks one gets from those stick-in-the-muds of Germans. No matter where you take them, they turn homesick on your hands for the flesh-pots of Egypt. The Doctor himself won't hold out for long.

CASPERLE.

What are you mumbling in your beard?

AUERHAHN.

How would you like to travel?

CASPERLE.

As quick as possible; the place might be filled up?

AUERHAHN.

I'll load a cannon with you, and shoot it off to Eigelstein.

CASPERLE.

All right, if it doesn't hurt; I don't care a button what happens if I'm not there.

AUERHAHN.

Well, it's not what one would call comfortable; so, I suppose, forsooth, I've got to convey you to Mainz on a sofa.

CASPERLE.

Done! but it must have spring stuffing.

AUERHAHN.

All right. [*A sofa appears, and on it sitting a beautiful young woman.*] Now, sit down. She won't eat you. Or, perhaps you're shy?

CASPERLE.

That's about it [*sings*] :

"For I'm such a bashful young man."

AUERHAHN.

Oh, yes! Hector it out. D'ye mean to say you don't know your own sister Dorothy?

CASPERLE.

Oh! It's Dorothy, is it? Oh! then I won't go.

YOUNG WOMAN.

Casperle ! Casperle !

CASPERLE.

" Dorothy ! Dorothy !
With a crooked shoulder ;
You passed away when young and gay,
And come back seven years older."

Off with you by yourself, I've had enough of you.

AUERHAHN.

Well, well, here's another travelling companion
for you. [*Sofa disappears, another comes, bearing
an old woman.*] Are you still shy ?

CASPERLE.

Oh ! The Devil's grandmother.

AUERHAHN.

No ! your own !

CASPERLE.

What ! Have you got her too ! Such a good old
lady, always read her daily lessons.

AUERHAHN.

Ah ! you can't trust the goodies.

OLD WOMAN.

Casperle ! Casperle !

CASPERLE.

A good journey to you ! You cuffed me over the
head too much with A B C. My brain is still
aching.

AUERHAHN.

If you won't travel with your own people, take the

Devil as our companion. [*Sofa, with old woman, disappears, other sofa, unoccupied, appears, on which* AUERHAHN *prepares to take a seat, but* CASPERLE *coming beforehand, stretches himself full-length on sofa, which carries him off to the clouds, leaving* AUERHAHN *on stage.*]

AUERHAHN.

The fellow's a match for three of us.

ACT IV.

SCENE I.

[*Street in Mainz. Right—House with carved figure of Madonna. Left—Hut,* CASPERLE'S *dwelling.*]

FAUST *alone—after* MEPHISTOPHELES.

FAUST.

Twelve years have passed away. I've searched the wide world o'er and found no joy, no gladness. The gold I caught at turned to dross when grasped. The foaming bowl of pleasure left bitter dregs behind; and how often was it snatched from my thirsty lips, as though I should here anticipate the tortures of the damned. If for such hollow mockery I bartered my eternal bliss, I was a fool, "a madman." The wide world I could no more endure. Uprooted from my home I seemed to wither and to fade, and now that homesick I return, every

familiar sight is a reproach. Here, I was once a
happy child that could believe and pray ; and why
can I pray no more? Because I cannot believe,
cannot? *Must* I not believe? Oh, that I were not
forced to do so by an unanswerable proof. If there
be a Devil there must be a God ; but this God I
have denied, abjured! Therefore I cannot pray ;
for prayer is Heaven's mercy, and for me there is
no mercy left. Oh, how I repent! Repentance!
Where that is, mercy is also found. Had I but
repentance aright, perhaps there might be mercy
even for me, a sinner. [*Sinks into meditation,*
MEPHISTOPHELES *touches him on shoulder*].

FAUST [*shuddering*].

What! You here !

MEPHISTOPHELES.

What's wrong? Are you turned sick or a monk ?
Why such a hang-dog mien? Once back again in
Mainz I thought the fun would be fast and furious ;
instead of that, you slink about like a whipped
hound. Often as you plagued me, working me to
death, paving the way for your carriage, bearing
you through the air, breaking through boards and
planks, and patching them up again behind you, did
I ever grumble at any task, however hard? Now,
however, I complain with justice, for you are turning
wearisome upon my hands, and a bore the Devil
himself cannot abide.

FAUST.

Leave me ! Disturb me not !

D

MEPHISTOPHELES.

Ah, but I will disturb you ; you must give me work.

FAUST.

Must I ?   Well then, listen !

MEPHISTOPHELES.

Say on.

FAUST.

Do you remember how by our compact you were bound to give true answer to each question I might choose to put ?

MEPHISTOPHELES.

I remember thinking you a fool for your pains in believing that Truth could be had from the Father of Lies.

FAUST.

If you fail in this condition, our bond is broken.

MEPHISTOPHELES.

I have never told you lies.

FAUST.

Hear, then, and give true answer to my question.

MEPHISTOPHELES.

Put your question.

FAUST.

Can I come to God ?

[MEPHISTOPHELES *quakes and trembles.*

FAUST.

The truth.

MEPHISTOPHELES [*stammering and whimpering*].

I know not.

FAUST.

Thou knowest! Answer, or our bond is *nil*. Can I come to God?

[MEPHISTOPHELES *disappears howling.* FAUST *falls upon his knees before the Madonna on the house.*

FAUST.

Thanks, Blessed Virgin, I am delivered and released. I can pray and weep once more. The stream of repentance is not wholly dried.

SCENE II.

FAUST. MEPHISTOPHELES. HELENA.

MEPHISTOPHELES.

Faust! cease to pray. 'Tis useless, because too late. Thou hast denied the God thou wouldst adore. One only hope now left is love, and true love you have never known ; that joy is yet in store. No woman e'er you saw was worthy of your heart, no, not the Duchess' self. Look upon her who only can return your love.

FAUST.

Leave me.

MEPHISTOPHELES.

Would you spurn her? The loveliest of earth and heaven. Know that she is Helena. That same Helena who turned every grey head in Troy.

FAUST.

Let me pray.

MEPHISTOPHELES.

You spurn her? Good! I take her back, and never more will Hades yield its treasure up, nor shall the sun shine again upon the loveliest of women.

FAUST.

Well, look at least I may. [*Looks up and rises from his knees.*] What symmetry! what perfection and what charm! Yes! she was worthy of the ten years' strife of the noblest of the nations! What happiness to call her all one's own.

MEPHISTOPHELES.

That happiness I offer you.

FAUST.

What! Is she mine? Ah, dare I call her mine? She, the noblest and the fairest of women seen on earth. Give her to me, that in her love I may have happiness supreme. Once blessed is blessed for ever. Give her! Give!

MEPHISTOPHELES.

Patience! Not so fast.

FAUST.

Why not? Give, I command you! Give her to me!

MEPHISTOPHELES.

First, you must again abjure Him whom you have just adored.

FAUST.

I abjure Him and for ever. With this treasure in my arms, I can defy both Him and you. Give!

MEPHISTOPHELES.

Take her.

[FAUST *enraptured, bears away* HELENA *to his house.*

MEPHISTOPHELES.

Ha! ha! ha! ha! Now you are mine. All the Saints of Heaven were powerless to save you. Ha! ha! ha! ha! A hot reception truly might I expect from my Lord did I let slip such easy prey.

FAUST [*bursting in wild frenzy out of the house*].

A curse upon you! A curse, I say! Vile, knavish arch-deceiver! I clasped a hellish serpent to my bosom. I would embrace her, and fell sickened and choked by the noisome pest that she breathed upon me. Is *that* your faithful service?

MEPHISTOPHELES.

Ha! ha! ha! ha! Cheating is my trade. Had you that yet to learn? Nor is this all; you are more befooled than yet you know!

FAUST.

Wretch! What would you say?

MEPHISTOPHELES.

The time is up. You have but a few hours left to live. At midnight you are mine.

FAUST.

What are you talking of? Have I not yet twelve years before me? Our compact was for four-and-twenty years at 365 days to the year.

MEPHISTOPHELES.

Poor dupe! So ignorant of the ways of Hell,

yet daring to enter into compact with it. You've
counted but the days. Have I not served the nights
as well, and thus in twelve years served the
promised twenty-four? At midnight, then, our
contract will expire. Notice!

[*Exit* MEPHISTOPHELES.

FAUST [*alone*].

Low pettifogger's quibble; but what if it should
hold? What if the hellish reading read aright?

HOLLOW VOICE FROM ABOVE.

[*Clock strikes Nine.*

Fauste! Fauste! Praepara te ad mortem.

[FAUST *rushes out, wringing his hands.*

SCENE III.

[CASPERLE *equipped as night-watch, with cloak,
staff and lantern, comes out of hut, whence a scolding
voice is heard.*]

CASPERLE.

All right, Gretl, you're wrong. She's just a pat-
tern wife, that of mine. Can't bear me to say she's
in the right. And isn't she right? Can't I light
my own lantern my own self? [*Lights lantern,
sings.*

"Good morning, pretty Lisa,
    The stars shine dark to-day,
So lend me if you please, a
    Lantern on my way."

Just so, now I'll sing something else.   [*Sings.*

" Ye gentlemen, hear one an' all,
   The clock strikes nine, just as I call,
   The clock strikes nine, the clock strikes nine !"
A little while ago, as I must confess, for my wife was scolding too loud for me to hear it. No matter. The gentry can sit the longer over their pint pots.

[*Sings.*

" Your lights put out, your fires put down,
   And so from harm preserve the town."
Now, who'd have thought that even a scolding wife can be of some good. The host shall pay me for being so late with police time, as he gets the profit.   [*Exit.*

SCENE IV.

FAUST. *Alone in street.*

FAUST.

" Praepara te ad mortem." But should we not always be prepared to die ? Perchance I did but dream the voice. Such are the terrors of awakened conscience, which, alas ! for long I have known too well. [*Clock strikes Ten. Counts.*] Ten o'clock ! Another hour is gone, an hour of torture, and yet all too quickly passed.

HOLLOW VOICE FROM ABOVE.

Fauste ! Fauste ! Accusatus es !

FAUST.

Woe ! woe is me ! 'Twas no imagination ! What shall I do and whither flee ? " Accusatus es."

Quid sum miser tunc dicturus
Quem patronum rogaturus?

Pray! Can I yet pray? Let me try. [*Kneels before Madonna on house.*] Virgo, Virginum praeclara. Oh, horror! The face becomes Helena's and heavenly devotion is quenched by earthly love. Satan! that is thine accursed craft. My heart defrauded of all earthly joys, cannot rise to those of Heaven. Is there, then, no mercy?

HOLLOW VOICE FROM ABOVE.

He, who on earth would God deny,
Is lost to all Eternity.

[FAUST *falls fainting to the ground.*

SCENE V.

FAUST. CASPERLE.

[*The latter again quarrelling with his wife; besides her voice is heard that of the child bawling at pitch of its voice, " Mother, father's giving me no porridge."*

CASPERLE [*coming out of hut with lighted lantern*].

[*Sings.*

" I'm glad I have no scolding wife,
There's not a greater plague in life."

But I *have* got a scolding wife. Now have I got one or not? *No,* I say. A scolding wife will have everything as her own head wags, whereas my wife makes my head the measure for everything. Chairs and tables, pots and pans, everything and anything, all come flying at it. [*To child, that goes on howling.*] Oh, bawl away! but porridge I won't give you. I've got my reasons : primo, I haven't time, as it's struck ten and duty comes before devotion. Pro secundo, Gretl's bitten my thumb. Prostertio, I haven't got any porridge, for Gretl didn't make any. [*Child screams "Father."*] Bawl away, I don't care. I've got my old song to sing again. [*Sings.*

"Hear one and all, good gentlemen,
The clock strikes ten, the clock strikes ten."
If I only knew which is good German. Das neuter clock or Der masculine ; some even say Die feminine clock, but that's nonsense ; in that case there would be no pendulum. [*Sings.*

"Put out your light, your fire put down,
And so from harm preserve the town.
The clock strikes ten, the clock strikes ten."
[*Stumbles over* FAUST.
Who lies there on the street ! He's as drunk as a lord ! That comes of police hours being so late, and that again from my wife's long tongue. Up, friend ! Up ! [FAUST *rises.*

CASPERLE.

Bless me ! If that isn't my old master who went to the Devil, and now he seems to have taken to the bottle ! I'll speak to him. Sir ! Don't you know me ?

FAUST.

No.

CASPERLE [*aside*].

That's all nonsense! He's just pretending not to know me because my wages are owing: rather mean. If I had so many Devils under my thumb, I wouldn't keep a poor beggar out of his money. [*Aloud.*] Then, Sir, you say you don't know me?

FAUST. No, indeed, who are you?

CASPERLE.

Why, who could I be but Casperle of course, to whom you are still owing six-and-thirty groschen wages, and twenty florins down, to drink; hard enough I earned them too, for I was nearly frightened to death by the Rat-tailed Devils and the ride on that infernal sparrow to Macaroniland, where you left me in the lurch and flew off with the ourangoutang to Stamboul. And before I could get home again there I had to sit—with weeping and wailing and gnashing of teeth.

FAUST.

With weeping and wailing and gnashing of teeth. Woe, woe is me!

CASPERLE.

I never looked to see you again. Thought the Devil had twisted your neck long ago. Still for all that, I didn't let the debt fly up the chimney, for often I needed the money, the drink tip especially; so now pay up to the last farthing, with interest and board wages into the bargain.

FAUST. Money? I have none.

CASPERLE.

Then for what in all the world did you give your poor soul to the Devil if you got no money?

FAUST.

Ah true! But money, I never thought of.

CASPERLE.

Paperlapap! That's what Wagner says and has it thick as hay! How could he treat the students to champagne, forsooth, if he hadn't money?

FAUST.

Wagner! Is he still here?

CASPERLE.

To be sure he is. Only yesterday we gave him a torchlight procession, on his promotion to "Magnificus"; a pretty penny it cost him, too. They drank three barrels "Oil de Perdrix." The expense nearly cost the old skinflint his wits.

FAUST.

Listen, Casperle. Money, I have none, but the buttons on my coat are worth your debt, ten times told over; so pay yourself by changing clothes with me. [Aside.] It is my first attempt at fraud, but I feel the knife already at my throat.

CASPERLE.

Oh, no! you're mighty clever, but Casperle too has a head on his shoulders. Suppose the wrong man were caught, I might find myself in the Devil's kitchen. Not for a thousand reichs-thalers would I stand in your shoes; you must have come to your last gasp to propose such a thing to me; I'll make

off as quick as I can, for the Devil's not over par-
ticular in his choice. [*Goes off, but returns.*] Look,
here's a bit of advice for you, if you're really afraid
of the Devil coming to fetch you. Do you see that
blue door; that's where my wife lives, just go in
and hide there, and there's not a Devil among them
that'll venture in after you; they're afraid of her.

SCENE VI.

FAUST *alone.* *After* MEPHISTOPHELES.

FAUST.

My last hope is gone. No escape is possible. I
am accused! But is sentence passed? Might I not
be acquitted? Eleven o'clock! I counted right.
                              [*Clock strikes Eleven.*

HOLLOW VOICE FROM ABOVE.

Fauste! Fauste! Judicatus es!

FAUST.

Woe! woe is me! Hell is my heritage. Yet
one hour more and the dread decree will pass; but
this torture that I now endure, is it not worse than
all the pains of Hell? I must have certainty.
Mephistopheles!

MEPHISTOPHELES.

What would you?

FAUST.

Tell me the truth, as bound, for still you are my
servant.

MEPHISTOPHELES.

What would you know?

FAUST.

My sufferings already here are terrible. Say!
Can those of Hell be yet more cruel still?

MEPHISTOPHELES.

That you shall learn full soon ; but if you will now
be told—know, that so exquisite are the pains of
Hell, that gladly would the poor damned souls climb
up a ladder of razors, if thereby they might escape
to Heaven.

[FAUST *buries his face in his hands
and rushes out.*

SCENE VII.

[*Sounds of quarrelling from hut. Blue door flies
open,* CASPERLE'S *Wife drives him out with a broom-
stick.*]

CASPERLE.

That's the thanks one gets for being hospitable.
I'm just too soft-hearted. There's my master owes
me wages and won't pay ; out of pity I yet offer him
the shelter of my house. No sooner does Gretl
hear that he comes to takes refuge with her from
the Devils that haven't courage to follow him in,
than she flies out in a fury, and takes to the broom-

stick.   But I'll pay her off when the clock strikes :
just wait.

     [*Clock strikes Eleven,* CASPERLE *sings.*
  " Now listen all,
   Both great and small,
   My wife has beat me sore ;
   So he, who's wise,
   He lives and dies
   A merry bachelor.
  Eleven o'clock !   Eleven o'clock !"

SCENE VIII.

FAUST.   DEVILS.

FAUST [*alone*].
 I am judged, and being judged, am condemned !
But—to what punishment?   How, if it were but to
Purgatory !   Awful hope, and *yet* a hope !
      [*Clock strikes Twelve.*
HOLLOW VOICE FROM ABOVE.
 Fauste ! Fauste !   In aeternum damnatus es !
FAUST.
 I am destroyed, annihilated !   Oh, that annihila-
tion were possible !

   [*Sinks to the ground, is seized and carried
    below by* DEVILS *in a shower of sparks.*
   CASPERLE *appears before his door.*

SCENE IX.

CASPERLE.

CASPERLE.

What's been going on here? Ugh! what a reek. Seems to have been an execution of infernal justice in honour of my old master, I fancy; always thought it would come to that at last. Pity though, that I hadn't known a little beforehand, I might have given him my compliments to take to grandmother.

[*Sings.*

" Good sirs, don't enter into evil
Communication with the Devil;
For in the end he's sure to cheat you,
And to a twisted neck to treat you.
The clock strikes twelve! The clock strikes
twelve."

Printed by BALLANTYNE, HANSON, & CO.
London and Edinburgh

www.ingramcontent.com/pod-product-compliance
Lightning Source LLC
Chambersburg PA
CBHW021535270326
41930CB00008B/1263